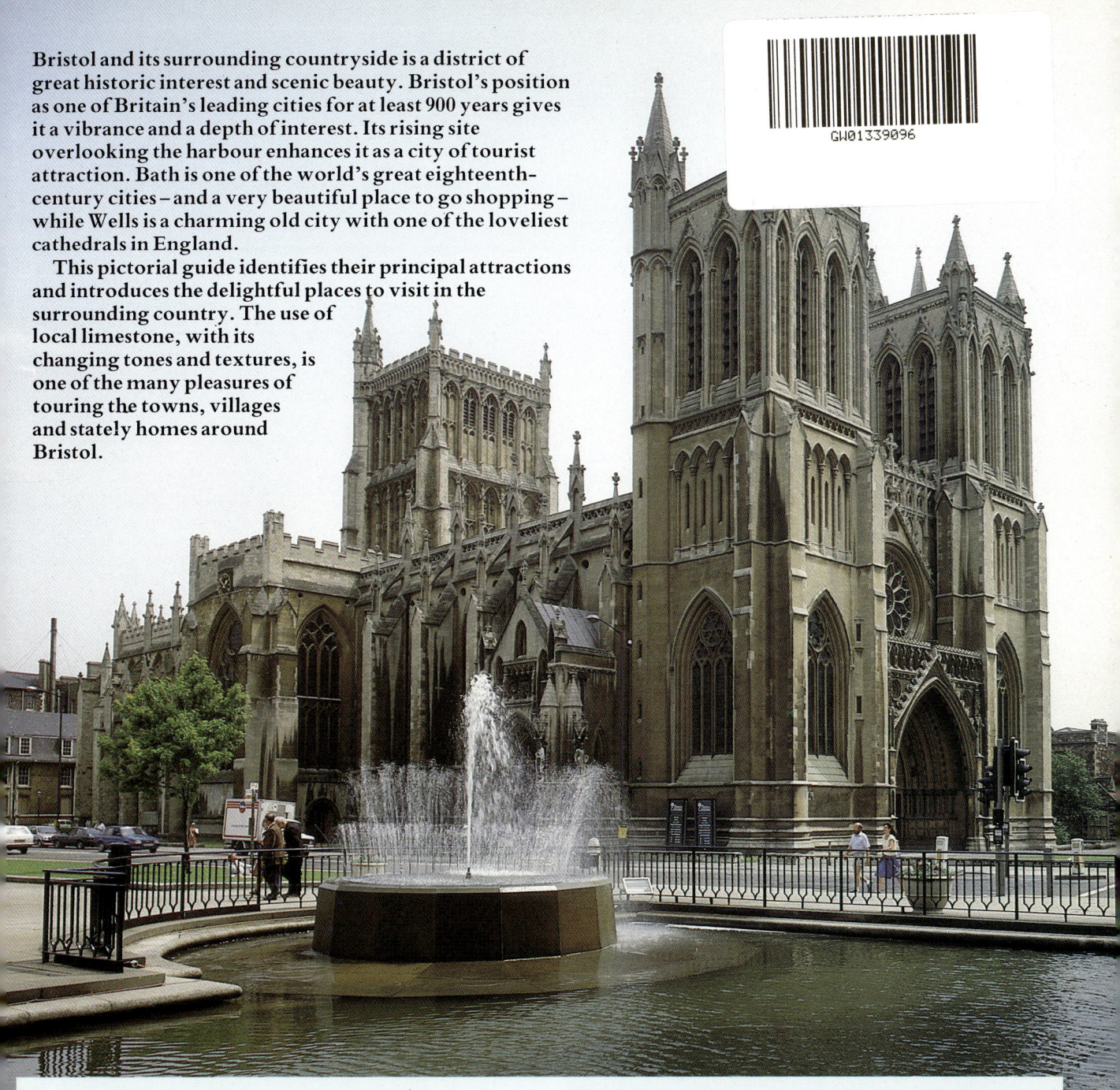

Bristol and its surrounding countryside is a district of great historic interest and scenic beauty. Bristol's position as one of Britain's leading cities for at least 900 years gives it a vibrance and a depth of interest. Its rising site overlooking the harbour enhances it as a city of tourist attraction. Bath is one of the world's great eighteenth-century cities – and a very beautiful place to go shopping – while Wells is a charming old city with one of the loveliest cathedrals in England.

This pictorial guide identifies their principal attractions and introduces the delightful places to visit in the surrounding country. The use of local limestone, with its changing tones and textures, is one of the many pleasures of touring the towns, villages and stately homes around Bristol.

Bristol und Umgebung ist eine Gegend von großem historischem Interesse und landschaftlicher Schönheit. Bristols Position als eine der führenden Städte seit mindestens 900 Jahren gibt der Stadt eine Resonanz und ein Interessenausmaß, das durch die ansteigende Lage mit Ueberblick über den Hafen, der Stadt als Touristenort eine große Anziehungskraft verleiht. Bath ist eine der Welts hervorragenden Städte der 18. Jahrhunderts – eine herrliche Stadt zum Einkaufen gehen – und Wells ist ein reizendes altes Städtchen mit einer der prächtigsten Kathedralen in England.

Dieser illustrierte Führer hebt die Hauptattraktionen dieser Städte hervor und berichtet über die besuchswerten Orte in der Umgebung. Eines der vielen Vergnügen, wenn man in den Städten, Dörfern und Historischen Häusern um Bristol herum spazieren geht, ist die Verwendung des lokalen Bausteins in seiner Gestaltung und den verschiedenen Farbtönen zu beachten.

Bristol et sa campagne environnante est une region d'un intérêt historique et touristique trés important. La position de Bristol en tant que l'une des villes les plus importantes de l'Angleterre depuis plus de 900 ans lui donne une vibration et profondeur certaine, ses sites élèves dominant le port en font également une ville touristique. Bath est une des plus importantes cités du XVIIIème siècle – et une trés jolie ville commerçante – alors que Wells est une charmante cité ancienne avec une des plus belles cathédrales en Angleterre.

Ce guide illustré présente les principales attractions de ces villes et introduit les ravissantes locations à visiter dans la campagne environnante. L'utilisation de la pierre locale avec ses couleurs changeantes est un des nombreaux plaisirs visuels recontrés lors de la visite de ces villes, villages et châteaux autor de Bristol.

Bristol is founded on the Rivers Avon and Frome, just six miles from the Bristol Channel. The early development of its harbour and the independent adventuring spirit of its citizens are the foundations of its history and riches.

By the fourteenth century, trade had made Bristol wealthy. Commerce was mainly with France and Spain, English cloth being traded for wines and iron. By 1497, with John Cabot's discovery of Newfoundland, Bristol was already looking westwards and in the seventeenth century religious and other refugees sailed from here to the New World, establishing valuable trading links.

Bristol became a centre for the Nonconformist community: in 1640 the first independent Baptist Congregation was founded at Broadmead; John Penn, a member of the city's Quaker community, founded Pennsylvania U.S.A. in 1681; and in 1739 John Wesley established his first church, which still exists in the Horsefair.

Bristol's prosperity continued in the eighteenth century, trading with the Americas in sugar, rum and tobacco, and in importance became second only to London. Ship-building and other industries (notably chocolate making and tobacco manufacture) flourished.

Isambard Kingdom Brunel is particularly connected with nineteenth-century Bristol: he designed Clifton Suspension Bridge, took a major part in planning the Great Western Railway and was the innovative designer of iron-clad and screw-propellor driven ships which were built in Bristol yards. However, the port declined. It was too shallow for modern ships and too far from the new centres of the Industrial Revolution. Throughout its history Bristol merchants have given generous patronage to the city, often in the form of buildings, a tradition which continues to this day.

At the heart of the city lies its Cathedral, *(photograph page 1)* built as an Augustinian Abbey in 1142 but refounded at the Dissolution of the Monasteries in 1542. From its earliest period are the Chapter House with fine late Norman decoration and the Elder Lady Chapel of early thirteenth-century date, which has delightful genre scenes carved by masons from Wells Cathedral. The early fourteenth-century Chancel is especially distinguished with its elegant and linear design, the thrust of the main vaults being carried across the aisles by horizontal members from which spring the aisle vaulting. To the south is the Berkeley Chapel, with a rare fifteenth-century brass candelabrum, and its ante-room with a flat stone ceiling supported on flying ribs, and succulent leaf carvings.

To the west is the Abbey's great Gateway, with Norman arches, and enlarged by Bishop Elyot in the 1520's — originally it led into the Abbey precinct. Alongside is the Central Library, a sensitive design of 1906 with a Tudor basis to compliment the Gatehouse, and a fine example of the Modern Movement. The large bland brick building facing down College Green is the Council House, *(photograph page 2)* the gilded unicorns on its roof being supporters from the city arms. Across the Green, a medieval window is a clue to the splendours of the Lord Mayor's Chapel, which is early thirteenth-century with a gilded ceiling of about 1500. Built for the Hospital of St. Mark, it was bought by the city at the Dissolution and in 1721 became the Chapel of the Mayor and Corporation, who still worship here. The sword-rest – made in 1702 by William Edney — is one of several in Bristol designed for holding the Lord Mayor's sword during worship.

College Green leads into Park Street, where smart shopping meets the University. Off Park Street and facing the Council House in College Street is Brunel House. Now offices, it was built in 1837 as the Royal Western Hotel, to a design by Brunel, primarily for passengers arriving from London by the Great Western Railway for an Atlantic crossing.

Bristol ist auf den Flüssen Avon und Frome gegründet worden, nur 10 km vom Bristol Kanal entfernt. Die frühe Entwicklung des Hafens und der unabhängige Unternehmungsgeist seiner Bewohner bilden die Grundlage seiner Geschichte und seines Reichtums.

Zur Zeit des 14. Jahrhunderts hatte sich Bristol durch den Handelsverkehr zu einer wohlhabenden Stadt entwickelt. Vorallem mit Frankreich und Spanien war der Verkehr rege; englischer Stoff wurde für Wein und Eisen gehandelt. Um 1497 begann Bristol durch John Cabots Entdeckung von Neufundland bereits nach dem Westen zu blicken und im 17. Jahrhundert begannen religiöse und andere Flüchtlinge von hier in die neue Welt zu segeln, wo sie wertvolle Handelsverbindungen herstellten.

Bristols Wohlergehen entwickelte sich im 18. Jahrhundert weiter im Handel mit Amerika in Zucker, Rum und Tabak und so stand die Stadt an Bedeutung nach London an zweiter Stelle. Der Schiffbau und andere Industrien (vorallem die Herstellung von Schokolade und die Verarbeitung von Tabak) gedeihten. Doch der Hafenverkehr verschlechterte sich. Für moderne Schiffe war der Hafen nicht tief genug und befand sich zu weit weg von den neuen Orten der industriellen Revolution.

Im Herzen der Stadt steht die Kathedrale (Foto Seite 1), erbaut im Jahre 1142 als eine augustinische Abtei, doch nach der Auflösung der Klöster ist sie im Jahre 1542 neu errichtet worden. Aus der frühesten Zeit stammen das Domkapital mit seinen feinen spät-normannischen Verzierungen und die Presbyter Marienkapelle von anfangs des 13. Jahrhunderts mit hübschen, von Steinhauern der Wells Kathedrale gemeißelten Genredarstellungen.

Der Kathedrale gegenüber, mit Blick zum College Green, steht ein großer Steinbau, Sitz der Stadtverwaltung (Foto Seite 2), wo man auf dem Dach vergoldete Einhörner, Halter des Stadtwappens, sehen kann. College Green führt zur Park Street, von wo man gepflegten eschäften entlang zur Universität gelangt.

Bristol a été fondée sur les rivières Avon et Frome, à environ six milles du Canal de Bristol. Le développement précoce de son Port ainsi que l'esprit indépendant et aventureux de ses citoyens sont à l'origine de l'histoire et des richesses de Bristol.

Dès le XIVème siècle, le commerce avait rendu Bristol riche. Le commerce se faisait principalement avec la France et l'Espagne, les étoffes anglaises étant negociées pour des vins et du fer. En 1497, avec la découverte du Nouveau Monde par John Cabot, Bristol se tournait déjà en direction de l'Ouest et au XVIIème siècle des réfugiés religieux et autres firent route sur le Nouveau Monde, établissant ainsi des liens commerciaux précieux avec Bristol.

La prospérité de Bristol a continué au XVIIIème siècle, avec le commerce du sucre, du rhum et du tabac avec les Amériques. Bristol devint la ville la plus importante après Londres. La construction navale et autres industries (notamment l'industrie du chocolat et du tabac) étaient en plein essor. Malgré tout cela l'importance du Port commença à décliner. Il n'était pas assez profond pour recevoir les navires modernes et trop éloigné des nouveaux centres de la Révolution Industrielle.

Au coeur de la Cité se trouve la Cathédrale (photo page 1), construite en 1142 comme une Abbaye Augustinienne mais refondée à la Suppression des Monastères en 1542. De la première période datent La 'Chapter House' (Maison des Chanoines) avec ses élégantes décorations romanes et la 'Elder Lady Chapel' (Chapelle de Lady Elder) datant du début du XIIIème siècle. Cette chapelle a de merveilleuses scènes sculptées par les maçons de la Cathédrale de Wells.

En face de la Cathédrale, le grand bâtiment en briques faisant face à 'College Green' est la 'Council House' (Hôtel de Ville) (photo page 2), les Licornes dorées sur son toit supportent les armoiries de la ville. 'College Green' donne sur la rue commerçante 'Park Street' qui mène à l'Université.

In Great George Street, still partly eighteenth-century, is the Georgian House built in 1789-91 for J.P. Pinney, a sugar merchant, and now on show furnished in period style. The street leads up to Brandon Hill, surmounted by the Cabot Tower (1897) built to commemorate John Cabot's voyage from Bristol and sighting of North America four hundred years earlier. It is indeed a proud Victorian tower, with an eccentric top-hamper, and panoramic views from the summit. Return by Charlotte Street, a lovely terrace of stone-faced houses built in 1787.

Crowning the view up Park Street is the University Tower, *(photograph page 5)* over two hundred feet high, a tour-de-force of late gothic design. The tower and adjoining buildings, completed in 1925, were given by Sir G.A. Wills and H.H. Wills of the tobacco company; they are among the earlier benefactions made by this family to the University, which received its charter in 1909.

The Victorian building next to the University Tower is the City Museum and Art Gallery *(photograph page 4)*. Its fine interior holds much local material, but its fame lies in its Oriental collection. Further up Queen's Road is the Royal West of England Academy (1854) with its original partly marble-lined interior, now used for art exhibitions. Facing it are the classical Victoria Rooms built in 1839; the pediment of their Corinthian portico displays figures representing Dawn. In front are a statue, fountains and sea beasts in bronze, commemorating Edward VII. The Rooms house the Bristol Exploratory, a new 'hands-on' exhibition of technological discoveries suitable for all ages!

The most interesting relic of sixteenth-century Bristol is Red Lodge, a small house built in about 1590 (with a later exterior) and now a period museum. The Large and Lesser Oak Rooms are quite exceptional, with good plaster ceilings and high quality panelling.

A hundred years later Edward Colston gave the almshouses named after him, in St. Michael's Hill; arranged around a square court, with oval and pedimented windows and a cupola, they are an early example of the classical style in Bristol. Below them are Foster's Almshouses (1861) in Colston Street, *(photograph page 5)*, a rebuilding of John Foster's Foundation of 1485, of which the stone Chapel of the Three Kings alone survives. The Victorian work is an attractive amalgam of Tudor and French gothic detail, of patterned brickwork with external galleries and a cylindrical staircase of timber. It backs onto Christmas Steps, *(photograph page 6)* a picturesque alley of miscellaneous houses, paved in 1669. At its lower end are the well-presented remains of St. Bartholomew's Hospital, founded in about 1200.

Höhepunkt des Ausblickes über Park Street ist der Universitätsturm (Foto Seite 5); er ist über 60 Meter hoch, ein Meisterwerk in spätgotischem Stil. Der im Jahre 1925 vervollständigte Turm und die angeschlossenen Gebäude waren Geschenke der Herren Sir G.A. Wills und H.H. Wills von der Tabakgesellschaft. Sie gehören zu den frühen Spenden dieser Familie an die Universität, der das Privileg im Jahre 1909 erteilt worden war.

Das neben dem Universitätsturm stehende viktorianische Gebäude ist das Stadt-Museum und die Gemäldegalerie (Foto Seite 4). Im prächtigen Innenraum befinden sich viele örtliche Gegenstände, berühmt ist jedoch vorallem die sich dort befindende orientalische Sammlung. Weiter der Queen's Road entlang ist die Royal West of England Akademie (1854) mit ihrer ursprünglichen, teilweise mit Marmor belegten Innenausstattung; heute wird die Akademie für Kunstausstellungen benützt. Ihr gegenüber sind die, im Jahre 1839 erbauten, klassischen Viktoria-Kammern, wo sich jetzt die, für jedes Alter geeignete, neue 'hands-on' Bristol Forschungs-Ausstellung über technologische Entdeckungen befindet.

Die Fosters Armenhäuser (1861) in Colston Street (Foto Seite 5) sind ein Umbau der John Foster Stiftung von 1485, wovon nur noch die Steinkapelle der Drei Könige besteht. Die viktorianische Arbeit ist eine hübsche Mischung von Tudor und französischer Gotik Ausführung mit gemusterter Maurerarbeit, Außen-Galerien und einem zylindrischen Treppenaufgang aus Holz. Nach hinten fällt der Blick auf Christmas Steps (Foto Seite 6), einen malerischen Durchgang mit verschiedenartigen Häusern und mit Pflasterung aus dem Jahre 1669.

Dominant 'Park Street' se trouve 'The University Tower' (La Tour de l'Université) (photo page 5), haute de plus de 200 pieds, elle est un tour de force de l'architecture gothique tardive. La tour et les bâtiments contigus terminés en 1925 ont été offerts à l'Université de Bristol par Messieurs G.A. Wills et H.H. Wills de la compagnie des tabacs. Ces donations sont parmi les premières faites par cette famille à l'Université qui reçu sa Chartre en 1909.

Le bâtiment de l'époque victorienne qui se trouve à côté de la Tour de l'Université est le 'City Museum' (Musée de la ville) et Galerie d'Art (photo page 4). Son élégant intérieur contient de nombreuses oeuvres d'art d'artistes locaux, mais le Musée est surtout connu pour sa collection orientale. Plus haut, dans la 'Queen's Road' (Rue de la Reine) se trouve le 'Royal West of England Academy' (Academie royale de l'Ouest de l'Angleterre) datant de 1854 avec ses interieurs d'origine partiellement marbrés qui maintenant abritent des expositions d'art. En face, se trouvent les classiques 'Victorian Rooms' (Salles de l'époque victorienne) datant de 1839. Dans ces salles se trouve le 'Bristol Exploratory', une nouvelle exposition sur les découvertes techniques pour tous les ages.

L'hospice Foster (1861) dans 'Colston Street' (photo page 5) est une reconstruction de la Fondation de John Foster de 1485, dont seule la Chapelle de pierre des Trois Rois a survecu. L'architecture victorienne est un attrayant amalgame de Tudor et de gothique francais avec galeries extérieures et un escalier cylindrique en bois. Par derrière, l'hospice donne sur les 'Christmas Steps' (Marches de Noël) (photo page 6), une allée pittoresque aux maisons diverses, pavée en 1669.

5

Corn Street is the grandest street in Bristol and owes its distinguished buildings to its role as the centre of eighteenth and nineteenth century finance. From the west, there are two fine banks on the south side (now Coutts and Barclays), Palladian buildings with excellent stonework of about 1840, then the Old Post Office (Mercantile Credit) pleasantly designed in 1746 with three bays and three storeys upon arches. Next is the Exchange built by John Wood the elder in 1741, extremely handsome and designed as a Palladian palace around a colonnaded square court. It still performs one of its original functions, housing market traders and now antique dealers too. Outside on the paving are the four Nails, brass balusters with flat tops and inscriptions of Elizabethan and Jacobean dates: before the Exchange was built payments were made here 'on the Nail' *(photograph page 7)*. Beyond is the Coffee House (1782), balancing the Old Post Office, and the baroque tower of All Saints' (1712) with a cupola added in 1807, another Bristol landmark. Opposite the Exchange is Lloyd's Bank, built in 1854 in a richly sculptured *seicento* Venetian style combining Bath and Portland stone. It stands next to the Old Council House, a Grecian building of 1822 by Sir Robert Smirke, with a pair of giant Ionic columns at the entrance and a seated figure of Justice enthroned on top.

Christ Church, at the corner of Broad Street, is internally the prettiest Georgian church remaining to Bristol after the terrible air-raid destruction of the last war. Built in 1786, its early Georgian style is modelled on St. Martin-in-the-Fields in London. The interior is ornate, with contemporary fittings, and a late seventeenth-century organ by Renatus Harris. Next in Broad Street come three nineteenth-century buildings of wildly contrasting styles and quality: C.R. Cockerell's superb Bank of England branch bank, with a deeply modelled facade of great refinement; next to it and exactly contemporary is the Guildhall, with grandiose late gothic detailing and a feeble tower, built in 1844; and the premises of Edward Everard, the craft printer, faced with coloured and glazed tiles, a period piece in the Art Nouveau style of 1900.

Facing up the street is St. John the Baptist's Church, built in the fourteenth century on top of the only remaining Gate in the City Walls; once the Walls supported three other churches. The nave was given by Walter Frampton, a merchant whose splendid effigy and tomb are here, and it has beautiful seventeenth-century furnishings such as the font and brass lectern. On the Gate are the figures of Brennus and Belinus, fabled as having founded Bristol.

Across Bristol Bridge lies Victoria Street, redeveloped during the boom of the 1860's. A few of its brash commercial buildings have survived both the blitz and recent redevelopment. St. Thomas's Church preserves some exceptional high-relief wood carvings including a reredos of 1716 and the organ gallery of 1728, precious relics of a type of work once common in Bristol. Victoria Street leads on towards the Great Western Railway Company's Temple Meads Station. The main hall was designed by Brunel in 1839, with a hammerbeam roof supported on concealed cast-iron pillars, the widest timber roofspan then existing. It is one of the very few structurally advanced buildings of Victorian Bristol and is also notable as a very early railway terminus comparatively unaltered.

Corn Street ist Bristols großartigste straße und verdankt seine hervorragenden Bauten der Rolle, die Bristol im 18. und 19. Jahrhundert als Finanzzentrum gespielt hat. Vom Westen her befinden sich zwei feine Banken an der Südseite (jetzt Coutts und Barclays), palladianische Bauten mit hervorragendem Mauerwerk von ca. 1840, und dann das alte Postamt (Mercantile Credit), ein hübscher Bau aus dem Jahre 1746.

Dann sieht man die äußerst stattliche Börse, die in 1741 von John Wood dem Aelteren als palladianischer Palast mit einem mit Säulengängen versehenen Innenhof erbaut worden ist. Dieses Gebäude behauste ursprünglich Markthändler, eine Rolle, die bis heute aufrecht erhalten worden ist und jetzt trifft man dort auch Antiquitätenhändler. Draußen auf dem Fußsteig sind 'die vier Nägel', Messingsäulen mit flachen Oberteilen und Inschriften von Daten aus den Zeiten Elisabeth I und Jakob I. Vor dem Bau der Börse wurden hier Zahlungen direkt gemacht, 'on the nail' (auf den Nagel) (Foto Seite 7).

'Corn Street' est la rue la plus grandiose de Bristol, elle doit ses élégants bâtiments à son rôle de centre financier au XVIII et XIXème siècle. En partant de l'Ouest, vous trouvez tout d'abord au sud, deux banques élégantes (maintenant Coutts et Barclays), des bâtiments palladiens avec une excellente maçonnerie datant de 1840, puis 'The Old Post Office' (Le vieux bureau de poste) agréablement dessiné en 1746.

Ensuite se trouve 'The Exchange' (La Bourse) construite en 1741 par John Wood père, d'une extrême élégance elle est réalisée dans le style d'un palais palladien autour d'une cour à colonnades. Elle remplit encore ses fonctions d'origine et héberge un marché et également des antiquaires. Dehors sur le trottoir, se trouvent quatre 'Clous', ballustres en cuivre à têtes plates avec des inscriptions datant de l'époque élisabethaine et jacobine. Avant que la Bourse ne soit construite, les paiements se faisaient là sur le clou, d'où l'expression 'to pay on the nail' ou 'payer rubis sur l'ongle'. (Photo page 7)

7

St. Mary Redcliffe (St. Mary on the red cliff of the Avon), *(photograph page 8)* and according to Queen Elizabeth I "The fairest, goodliest and most famous parish church in England", is of cathedral-like ambitions. It was rebuilt steadily through the fourteenth and fifteenth centuries to one exceptionally refined design, which gives it a wonderful unity. Throughout it has vaulting above a tall clerestory, necessitating the graceful flying buttresses; and the church is full of small-scale sculptures of the highest quality — including some twelve hundred vaulting bosses. There is a monument to Sir William Penn, adorned with his armour. He died in 1670 and Pennsylvania U.S.A. is named after him. Another American memento is a whale's rib in the tower, brought back by Cabot from discovering Newfoundland in 1487-8.

Across the Avon stands the Granary on Welsh Back (1869), which has been called 'the most striking and piquant monument to the high Victorian age in Bristol'. It has ten storeys treated as six, with patterned brickwork of greatly varied detail, and Venetian battlements. Nearby is Queen's Square, a landmark in Bristol's architectural development. Begun in 1699, it established the popularity of brick and sash windows, both then new to the city. Bristol's earliest square, its seven acres made it also the second largest in England. The best houses are on the south side, no. 29, built in 1709-11, having three Orders of columns and 'grotesque' carved heads above the windows. The original north and west sides were largely burned in the Reform Riots of 1831. The bronze statue in the centre of the square was sculpted by Rysbrack in 1732-6 and lays claim to be the finest equestrian statue in England.

Almost adjacent is King Street, established on the southern flank of the City Wall in 1650, and still cobbled. At the west end the Merchant Venturers' Almshouses, founded in the fifteenth century for retired seamen, were rebuilt by the generosity of Edward Colston in 1696-9; the inscription-board is worth reading. Next door is the dignified Old Library, where the poets Coleridge and Southey once worked. Rebuilt in 1740, it was founded in 1613 and is the second oldest public library in England. Further along the tall-arched brick building (Building Centre) originated as a cork warehouse in 1870. Next is the Cooper's Hall, built in 1743 and now the foyer of the Theatre Royal run by the Bristol Old Vic Company. The larger auditorium is the original theatre begun in 1764, which makes it the oldest playhouse in existence. The design was approved by David Garrick, and Sarah Siddons, Henry Irving and Ellen Terry have all acted here. At the corner is the multi-gabled St. Nicholas's Almshouse of 1652.

The fine three-storey house with the shell-hood opposite dates from about 1710. Also on the south side is the 'Llandoger Trow', *(photograph page 10)* built in the 1660's as a terrace of five houses, but shortened to three in the blitz. This inn is said to be the original of the 'Admiral Benbow' in R.L. Stephenson's Treasure Island.

St. Mary Redcliffe (St. Mary auf der roten Klippe des Avon Flusses) (Foto Seite 8), gemäss Königin Elisabeth I 'Englands schönste, stattlichste und berühmteste Kirche' ist im Streben einer Kathedrale ännlich. Sie wurde durch das 14. und 15. Jahrhundert hindurch ständig nach einem außerordentlich feinentworfenen Plan erbaut und das vollendete Werk zeigt eine wunderbare Einheit. Durch die ganze Kirche hindurch sind Wölbungen über einem hohen Lichtgaden, was die graziösen Strebebögen erforderlich macht. Ueberall sind verkleinerte, hochgradige Skulpturen, einschliesslich etwa zwölfhundert Gewölbebossen.

Der King Street entlang ist die Cooper's Hall, die im Jahre 1743 erbaut worden ist und jetzt als Foyer des Königlichen Theaters dient. Das Theater wird von der 'Bristol Old Vic Company' geführt. Das größere Auditorium ist das ursprüngliche Theater, welches bis zum Jahre 1764 zurückreicht und somit das älteste bestehende Schauspielhaus ist. Auf dem Wege zum Fluß ist der 'Llandoger Trow' (Foto Seite 10), *erbaut in den 1660er Jahren als eine aus fünf Häusern bestehende Reihe, die dann im Blitzkrieg zu drei Häusern verkürzt wurde. Es heißt, dies sei der Originalgasthof 'Admiral Benbow' in der 'Treasure Island' Geschichte von R.L. Stephenson.*

St Mary Redcliffe (St Mary sur la colline rouge de l'Avon) (photo page 8) *d'après la Reine Elizabeth I, l'église paroissiale la plus belle, la plus large et la plus connue de toute l'Angleterre est de l'envergure d'une cathédrale. Elle fut reconstruite durant le XIV et XVème siècle suivant un dessin exceptionnellement raffiné qui lui procure une merveilleuse* unité. Elle est pleine de voûtes au dessus d'une haute claire — voie, nécessitant les gracieux arcs boutants. L'église est pleine de petites sculptures de haute qualité comprenant environs 1200 bosses de voûtes.

Dans 'King Street' (La rue du Roi) se trouve le 'Cooper's Hall', construit en 1743 il héberge maintenant le Théâtre Royal dirigé par la 'Bristol Old Vic Cie'. L'auditorium le plus large est à l'emplacement du premier théâtre, commencé en 1764, il est le plus ancien théâtre en existence. En approchant de la rivière on trouve le 'Llandoger Trow, (photo page 10) construit en 1660, il était formé de cinq maisons dont trois seulement ont survécu après les bombardements. Il est dit que cette auberge est celle de l'Amiral Benbow dans le livre de R.L. Stephenson, "l'Ile aux trésors".

St. Augustine's Reach was dug in the 1240's to enlarge Bristol's harbour, and it is now lined with nineteenth and twentieth century commercial buildings, many of them converted recently to leisure uses including the Watershed *(photograph page 11)*. From the Arnolfini Gallery, a well-known contemporary arts centre, housed in a tea warehouse of 1832, you may cross the Floating Harbour on a turntable bridge to Prince's Wharf. Here are the National Lifeboat Museum and the Bristol Industrial Museum, displaying full-scale turbine engines and a model of a Concorde pilot's cabin. A short walk to the west, in Great Western Dock where she was built in 1843, is the S.S. Great Britain, *(photograph pages 12/13)* the first screw-propellor driven iron ship, designed by Brunel. The Maritime Heritage Centre adjacent *(photograph page 11)* is an excellent introduction to both the Great Britain and Bristol's maritime past.

'St. Augustine's Reach' (Kanalabschnitt) wurde um 1240 gegraben, um den Bristol Hafen zu vergrössern. Dort stehen jetzt Handelshäuser des 19. und 20. Jahrhunderts, wovon einige vor kurzem zu Freizeitgestaltungszwecken umgewandelt worden sind, wie z.B. 'The Watershed' (Foto Seite 11). Von der Arnolfini Galerie, einem bekannten modernen Kunstzentrum, dessen Behausung ein in 1832 erbautes Teehandelshaus ist, kann man den 'schwimmenden Hafen' auf einer Drehscheibenbrücke zum Prince's Landungssteg überqueren. Hier findet man das nationale Lifeboat (Rettungsboot) Museum und das Bristol Industrie-Museum, wo man vollständige Turbinenwerke sowie ein Modell der Pilotenkabine eines Concordes besichtigen kann. Nach einem kurzen

Spaziergang in westlicher Richtung kommt man zum Great Western Dock und dem Schiff 'Great Britain' (Foto Seite 12). Dieses Schiff wurde hier in 1843 gebaut. Es ist das erste Schiff aus Eisen mit Propellerantrieb und ist von Brunel entworfen worden. Im nebenanliegenden Maritime Heritage Zentrum (Foto Seite 11) kann man eine ausgezeichnete Einführung in die Geschichte des 'Great Britain' sowie in Bristols Seehandelsvergangenheit erhalten.

'St. Augustine Reach' a été creusé en 1240 pour élargir le port de Bristol, il est maintenant flanqué de bâtiments commerciaux datant du XIX et XXème siècle, plusieurs de ces bâtiments ont récemment été convertis en centre de loisirs, ex: 'le Watershed' (photo page 11). A partir de la Galerie Arnolfini, centre réputé des arts contemporains, installée dans un ancien entrepôt datant de 1832, vous pouvez traverser le port par un pont tournant qui vous mènera au 'Prince's Wharf' (Embarcadère du Prince). Sur ce quai se trouvent le Musée National des Bateaux de Sauvetage et le Musée Industriel de Bristol exposant des moteurs à turbine grandeur réelle et un modèle de la cabine de pilotage du Concorde. En marchant un peu vers l'ouest, dans 'Great Western Dock', se trouve 'S.S. Great Britain' (photo page 12), le premier navire à hélice, dessiné par Brunel et construit en 1843 dans ce bassin. Le 'Maritime Heritage Centre' (Centre de l'héritage maritime) (photo page 11) est une excellente introduction au passé maritime de la Grande Bretagne et de Bristol.

Clifton is an attractive area on rising ground to the west of the city centre, *(photograph page 15)* with graceful terraces and crescents developed between 1790 and 1850, with one eye on Bath, together with a few fine villas of earlier date. There are many attractive walks to be had around its curving streets, with marvellous views over the city and docks. Particularly fine are Windsor Terrace (1793) with giant Corinthian pilasters, and Royal York Crescent *(photograph page 15)* built in 1810-20.

Clifton's most renowned monument is the Suspension Bridge, *(photograph centre pages)* built with money donated in 1752 and designed in 1831 by Brunel, who wanted it to be "as simple and unobtrusive as possible" and to have the appeal of the sublime. Nearby on the Down stands the Observatory, a camera obscura in a 'medieval' tower built in 1829. Climb up and see a panoramic image of Bristol reflected before you. Bristol Zoo in Clifton Down Road, has large numbers of fish, fowl and beasts attractively housed in landscaped gardens, and includes a delightful collection of small nocturnal animals.

To the south-west of Bristol is Ashton Court, an elegant mansion of several dates and home of the Smyth family of Bristol merchants from 1545 until 1960. The estate is now being developed as a centre for outdoor recreations such as ballooning, *(photograph page 14)* riding and golf. Our visit to Bristol ends here and moves into the countryside.

Westlich von Stadtzentrum sind die Anhöhen der anziehenden Clifton Gegend (Foto Seite 15). Hier sieht man hübsche Häuserreihen und halbmondförmige Straßen aus der Zeit von 1790-1850 und im Stil von Bath beeinflusst; auch stehen hier noch einige schöne Villen aus früheren Zeiten. Man kann viele angenehme Spaziergänge machen und hat eine wunderbare Aussicht über die Stadt und die Docks. Hervorragend sind vorallem Windsor Terrace (1793) mit den riesigen korinthischen Pilastern und Royal York Crescent (Foto Seite 15) erbaut in 1810-1820.

Cliftons best bekanntes Monument ist jedoch die Hängebrücke (Foto Mittelseiten), erbaut aus im Jahre 1752 erhaltenen Gaben und von Brunel in 1831 entworfen. Brunel wollte eine möglichst einfache und unaufdringliche Brücke, die jedoch den Eindruck von Erhabenheit machte. Bristol war durch das 19. Jahrhundert hindurch besonders verbunden mit Brunel, denn er spielte eine ganz bedeutende Rolle in der Planung der 'Great Western Railway'.

Im Südwesten von Bristol ist Ashton Court, eine elegante Herrenhaus. Der Besitz wird jetzt als Freizeitbeschäftigungsplatz entwickelt und außer reiten und Golf-spielen kann man nun auch Ballon-fliegen (Foto Seite 14). Hier endet unser Besuch nach Bristol und wir gehen weiter in die umgebende Landschaft.

Clifton est un joli quartier situé sur la hauteur à l'ouest du centre de Bristol (photo page 15), on y trouve d'élégantes alignées de maisons et des rues en forme d'arc de cercle appelées 'croissants' construites entre 1790 et 1850, on y trouve également des petites maisons ou villas plus anciennes. Il y a de nombreuses et agréables promenades à faire le long des rues tortueuses, avec des vues merveilleuses sur la ville et les bassins du port. La 'Windsor Terrace' (1793) (photo page 15) avec ses pillastres corinthiens et le 'Royal York Crescent' construit en 1810-1820, (photo page centrale) sont de trés beaux examples de l'élégante architecture recontrée à Clifton.

Mais le monument le plus réputé de Clifton est certainement le 'Suspension Bridge' (Pont suspendu) (Photo page 16) dessiné par Brunel en 1831 et construit grâce à des dons financiers reçus en 1752. L'idée de Brunel était de construire un pont aussi simple et discret que possible tout en lui donnant une allure sublime. Brunel est particulièrement associé avec le Bristol du XIXème siècle, il a joué un rôle important dans le projet de construction du 'Great Western Railway' (Le Grand Chemin de Fer de l'Ouest).

Au sud — ouest de Bristol se trouve 'Ashton Court', un élégant palais dont la propriété est actuellement développée en centre de loisirs. Les ballades en ballon, les randonnées équestres et le golf peuvent y être pratiqués. Ici s'achève notre visite de Bristol et nous allons maintenant visiter la campagne environnante.

15

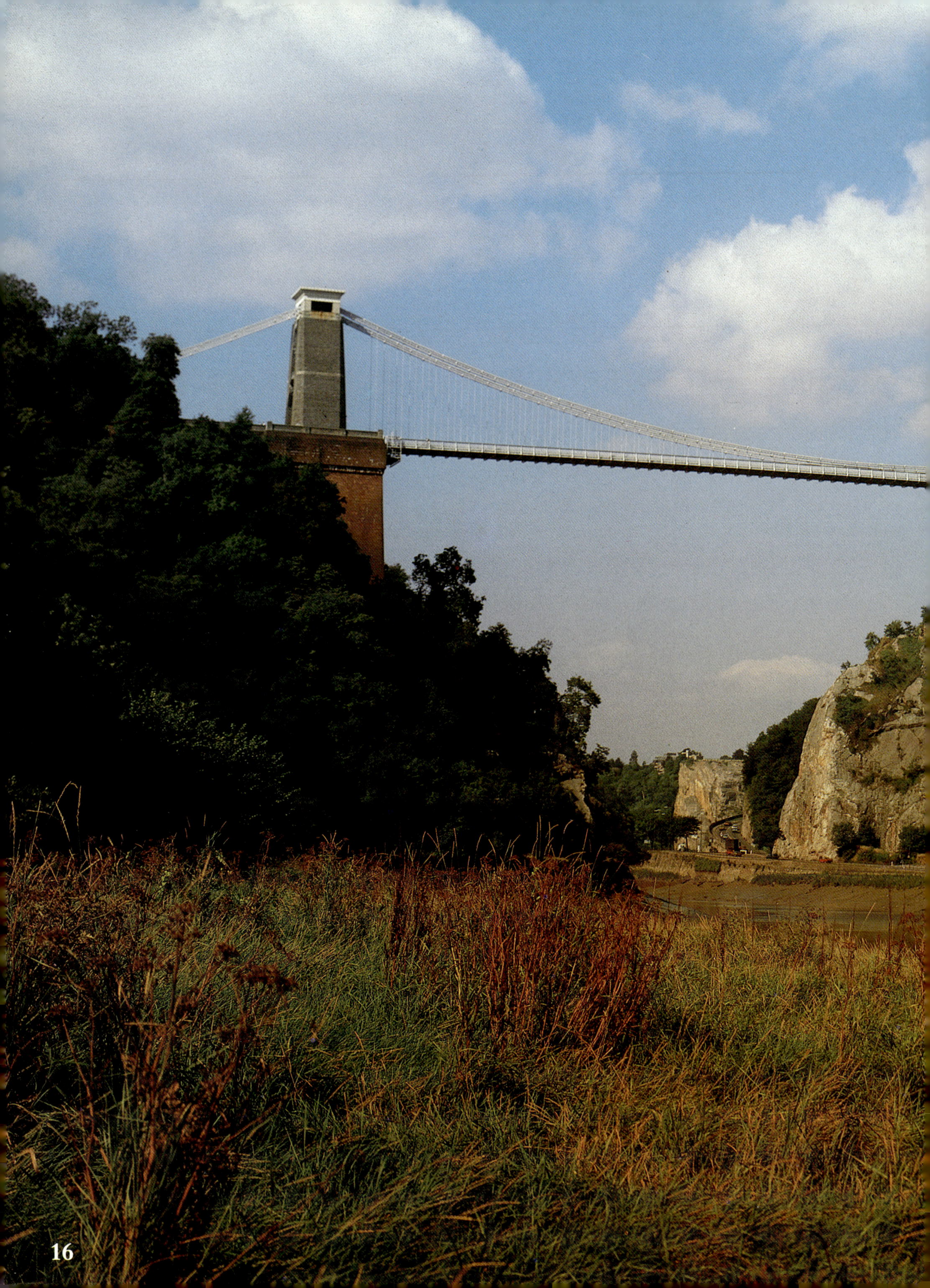

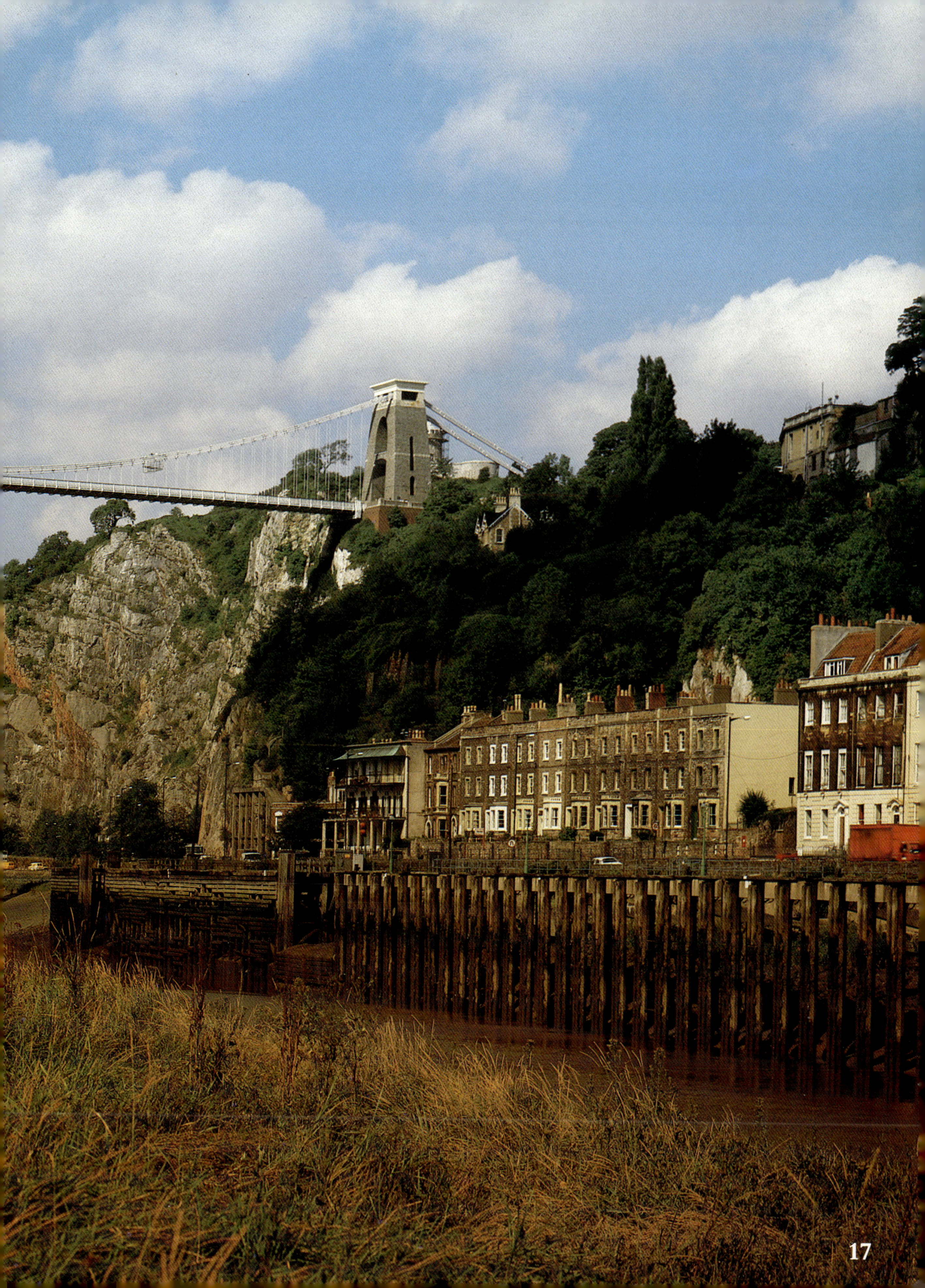

South of Bristol, near Wells, lies Wookey Hole in the Mendips, *(photograph page 18)* an impressive chain of caves cut out of Dolomitic conglomerate rock by the action of the river Axe. Nine of them can be visited, including Hell's Passage and the Witch's Kitchen, Hall and Parlour, named after a witch who was believed in the Middle Ages to live there and eat the local children. The stalactites and stalagmites vary in colour according to the minerals dissolved in the calcite.

Appended to the caves are a demonstration of hand-making paper and Lady Bangor's collection of Victorian and Edwardian fairground equipment.

Nearby are the Cheddar Caves, set in the glorious scenery of Cheddar Gorge *(photograph page 19)* and near the town which gave its name to the cheese. Their mineral growths are partly translucent, while others produce a musical note when struck.

Wells is a small country town, which knew great prosperity in the Middle Ages. At its centre lies the Market Place and on one side there is a row of three-storey shops, which are typical of Wells: pretty frontages, here Georgian with their sash and bay windows, but added to properties built in the fifteenth century, by Bishop Bekynton. There are also two gatehouses leading from the Market Place, both works of Bishop Bekynton. One of them is called the Bishop's Eye and leads to the Bishop's Palace, a group of partly ruinous stone buildings within a walled moat, built mainly in the thirteenth century. In addition to their great architectural interest, telling us much about medieval bishop's palaces, their picturesque qualities are enhanced by the beautiful setting of lawn, trees and moat *(photograph page 22)*.

Im Süden von Bristol, in der Nähe von Wells, liegt in den Mendips Hügeln Wookey Hole (Foto Seite 18). Wookey Hole besteht aus einer Reihe von Höhlen, die durch die Wirkung des Flusses Axe aus den dolomitischen Konglomeratfelsen geformt worden sind. Man kann neun davon besichtigen. Gemäß einer Legende wohnte im Mittelalter eine Hexe dort, die die Kinder der Gegend aufaß und dadurch erhielten die Höhlen Namen wie Höllengang, Hexenküche, Saal und Stube.

Von den Höhlen führt ein Weg in eine alte Papierfabrik, wo man einer Vorführung für handgemachtes Papier beiwohnen kann. Danach steht die Lady Bangor Kollektion viktorianischer und eduardischer Karussell- und Messe-Ausstattungen zur Schau.

Nicht weit entfernt befinden sich die Cheddar Höhlen in der prächtigen Cheddar Gorge Landschaft (Foto Seite 19) in dem kleinen Ort, nach dem der Cheddar Käse genannt ist. Die Mineralentwicklungen in den Höhlen sind teilweise lichtdurchlässig und gewisse erzeugen beim Anschlagen musikalische Töne.

Wells ist eine kleine Landstadt, die im Mittelalter groß en Wohlstand genoß. Mitten im Städtchen ist der Marktplatz (Foto Seite 19). Im Platz stehen zwei Torhäuser, die beide vom Bischof Bekynton erstellt worden sind. Das eine heißt 'the Bishop's Eye' (das Auge des Bischofs) und führt zum Bischofspalast, einer Gruppe von teilweise baufälligen, hauptsächlich aus dem 13. Jahrhundert stammenden Gebäuden, innerhalb eines ummauerten Wassergrabens. Abgesehen von der großen architektonischen Bedeutung und der Belehrung über mittelalterliche Bischofspaläste ist der Sitz mit seinen Rasen, Bäumen und dem Burggraben ein Ort von großer Schönheit.

Wells Cathedral

Au sud de Bristol, près de Wells, dans les Mendips se trouve 'Wookey Hole' (Le gouffre de Wookey) (Photo page 18), une impressionnante chaine de caves creusées dans de la roche conglomérée dolomitique par la rivière Axe. On peut visiter neuf de ces caves, dont 'Hell's Passage' ou Passage du Diable, la Cuisine, l'Entrée et le Salon de la Sorcière nommée après une sorcière qui au moyen-age était supposée habiter dans ces caves et manger les enfants du pays.

A côté des caves se trouve un atelier dans lequel est démontrée la fabrication manuelle du papier, et une pièce avec la collection d'équipement de fête foraine datant de l'époque victorienne et édouardienne appartenant à Lady Bangor.

Tout près se trouvent les Caves de Cheddar, situées dans le merveilleux paysage des Gorges de Cheddar (Photo page 19), à côté de la ville qui a donné son nom au fromage. Leurs croissances minérales sont partiellement translucides alors que d'autres produisent une note musicale lorsqu'on les frappe.

Wells est une petite ville de province qui a connu une grande prospérité au Moyen-Age. Au centre se trouve la 'Place du Marché' (Photo page 19). Il y a deux loges donnant sur la Place du Marché, toutes les deux ont été édifées par l'évêque Bekynton. L'une de ces loges est appelée 'The Bishop's Eye' (l'Oeil de l'Evêque) et mène au Palais épiscopal, un groupe de bâtiments pratiquement en ruines entourés de douves, construit au XIIIème siècle. En plus de leur intérêt architectural et le fait qu'ils renseignent sur les palais épiscopaux de l'époque médiévale, leurs qualités pittoresque sont rehaussées par un bel environnement de pelouses, abres et douves.

19

The smaller gatehouse is Pennyless Porch, which leads to Cathedral Green. Wells Cathedral was rebuilt in the early Gothic style in 1180-1240, and Decorated style in 1290-1340, on the site of an earlier cathedral.

The earlier period is seen at its best within the nave, a beautifully balanced piece of work, and in the north porch, always the main entrance. The emphasis is on harmonious design and bringing the surfaces to life. The west facade, recently restored, is moved by a completely different spirit and is presented as a screen of complicated shape for innumerable sculptures, of which nearly four hundred survive; in the Middle Ages they were brightly painted and gilded!

The Decorated work concerns the chancel and everything to the east of it. It is among the most imaginative architecture of its date in Europe, with exciting spatial effects, the development of new tracery patterns and a generous use of mouldings. The chapter house, up a flight of well-trodden steps, has vaulting thick with mouldings, and at the centre is what has rightly been called 'the finest cone of ribs in England'. Perfectly crowning the whole Cathedral is the central tower, a masterpiece by any standard. Its huge weight led to the strainer arches being inserted about twenty years later, in 1340. Enormously bold in conception, they deliberately disrupt all views within the Cathedral, while having a distinct grandeur of their own. Their uncompromising spirit is characteristic of this period at Wells *(photograph page 20)*.

Within, there are many details of interest, including the famous clock in the north transept, of 1390. Rings on the dial rotate to give the date, hour and minute, the phases of the moon are shown, and four mounted figures above spin round on the hour *(photograph page 21)*.

Back on Cathedral Green, there is another medieval gatehouse and several large houses, one now the Wells Museum. Originally the Dean and senior members of his Chapter lived here. Further along is the stone-vaulted Chain Gate, with a handsome gallery over it. This was built across the road in the fifteenth century to connect the Hall of the Vicars, who sang all the services, with their Cathedral. The Vicars had been given their own Close, on the left, by Bishop Ralph in 1348; it has forty-two houses with the Vicars' Hall at one end and their library and chapel at the other.

Das kleinere Torhaus heißt 'Pennyless Porch' (Pfenniglose Halle) und führt auf den Rasen vor der Kathedrale. Die Kathedrale von Wells wurde auf der Stelle einer früheren Kathedrale um 1180-1240 im früh-gotischen Stil und um 1290-1340 im englisch-gotischen Stil erbaut. Der Mittelturm, ein Meisterwerk in jeder Hinsicht, krönt die ganze Kathedrale. Das enorme Gewicht erforderte 20 Jahre später um 1340 das Einsetzen von Scherenbögen. Dieser äußerst kühne Entwurf verleiht eine gewisse Grossartigkeit, doch verloren war damit, wohl absichtlich, Uebersicht über die ganze Kathedrale. Der unbeugsame Eindruck, der diese Bögen verleiht, ist ein Merkmal jener Zeiten in Wells (Foto Seite 20).

Im Innern der Kathedrale gibt es viel Interessantes zu sehen. Im nördlichen Querschiff is eine Uhr aus dem Jahre 1390. Das Zifferblatt zeigt nicht nur die Stunde und Minute, sondern auch das Datum, die Mondphasen und zudem kreisen jede Stunde vier berittene Figuren herum (Foto Seite 21).

8 km von Wells entfernt liegt Glastonbury, ein Ort, wo sich ein Reichtum an Geschichte und Legenden wunderbar und unauflösbar verbunden hat. Ob Joseph von Arimathea den heiligen Grol auf dem Chalice Hügel begraben hat oder nicht, und ob der heilige Dornbusch, der hier an verschiedenen Stellen wächst, von seinem Stab herrührt oder nicht, als sicher wird angenommen, daß das Christentum in Großbritannien in Glastonbury begonnen hat. Von der Abtei (Foto Seite 23) sieht man noch die Ruinen der großen Kirche und der St. Mary's Kapelle mit den Steinhauerwerken des 12. Jahrhunderts, alles erbaut nach einem Brand des ursprünglichen Baues in 1184. Es heißt, daß im Altarsplatz die Leichen von König Arthur und Königin Guinevere begraben sind, nachdem Mönche sie im Jahre 1191 dorthin gebracht hatten.

La plus petite loge appelée 'Pennyless Porch' donne sur 'Cathedral Green'. La Cathédrale de Wells fut reconstruite dans le style gothique en 1180-1240, et décorée en 1290-1340, sur, l'emplacement d'une première cathédrale. Couronnant parfaitement toute la Cathédrale est la tour centrale qui est un véritable chef—d'oeuvre. Son énorme poids a entraîné l'insertion de voûtes, vingt ans plus tard, en 1340. Très grossières dans leur concept, elles dérangent la vue à l'intérieur de la Cathédrale tout en ayant une grandeur personnelle distincte. Leur dessin sans compromis est caractéristique de cette époque à Wells (Photo page 20).

A l'intérieur de la Cathédrale on trouve de nombreux détails intéressants telle la fameuse horloge dans le transept septentrional (1390). Des cercles sur le cadran tournent pour donner la date, l'heure et la minute, les phases lunaires sont également montrées et quatre figurines à cheval pivotent à chaque heure (Photo page 21).

A cinq milles de Wells, se trouve Glastonbury, ville merveilleusement riche en faits historiques et légendes qui se mélangent presque inextricablement. Est-il vrai que Joseph d'Arimathie a enterré le Saint Graal dans la colline Calice et est-il vrai que le Buisson épineux sacré qui pousse en plusieurs endroits est le descendant des disciples? Glastonbury est la fondation chrétienne la plus ancienne en Grande Bretagne. De l'Abbaye (Photo page 23) il ne reste que les ruines de l'énorme église et de la Chapelle St. Mary, avec ses riches sculptures du XIIème siècle, toutes refaites après qu'un feu est dévasté les bâtiments d'origine en 1184. On dit que dans le Choeur reposent le Roi Arthur et la Reine Guinevere, les moines les y auraient transportés en 1191.

Five miles from Wells lies Glastonbury, wonderfully rich in history and legends, which blend almost inextricably. Whether Joseph of Arimathea buried the Holy Grail in Chalice Hill and whether or not the Holy Thorn which grows in several places is the descendant of his staff, Glastonbury is accepted as the oldest Christian foundation in Britain. William of Malmesbury observed in 1125 that a church built of wattles, called the Old Church in 633, had a mystique of great holiness.

Of the Abbey, *(photograph page 23)* there remain the ruins of the huge church and of St. Mary's Chapel, with its rich twelfth-century carvings, all built after a fire which burned the original buildings in 1184; in the chancel are said to lie the bodies of King Arthur and Queen Guinevere, transferred there by the monks in 1191. Nearby, the Abbot's private kitchen is one of the grandest medieval kitchens in Europe.

The most prominent feature at Glastonbury is the Tor, a conical hill 520 feet high, crowned by the tower of St. Michael's Church. It must be climbed, if only for the view.

Near Warminster to the south-east of Bristol is Longleat, the great house of the Thynne family, Marquesses of Bath, to whom it still belongs. Built by Sir John Thynne, mainly in the 1570's, it is remarkably little altered externally. Longleat is the apogee of Elizabethan architecture, self-confident, with a distinguished appearance and a judicious use of the new renaissance detail, harmonious and symmetrical elevations, huge windows and an interesting skyline, all in the crispest of stone. The most exciting approach is the descent from the east through Capability Brown's landscaped park, with its trees planted in 1752-62, and distant views of the house and its roofscape.

Within, there is Sir John's hall, with hammerbeam roof trusses and carved pendants, but elsewhere the interior is mainly in an opulent Italian style of the 1870's, with much fine craftsmanship and ornate and highly coloured detail which provides a magnificent setting for the house's fabulous contents.

There are numerous other attractions at Longleat, including the Wildlife Park and its lions.

Corsham, south-west of Chippenham, is a town very rich in varied buildings of the seventeenth and eighteenth centuries, built of golden limestone, and well repays a little exploration.

Corsham Court was built in 1582 by Thomas Smythe, Collector of the Customs of London, and acquired in 1745 by Paul Methuen, to whose descendant it still belongs. The Methuen ownership has seen several major alterations to provide fine rooms suitable for their distinguished paintings, by such masters as Van Dyck, Rubens, Poussin, Filippo Lippi, Reynolds, Gainsborough and Romney. *(photograph of Picture Gallery page 23)*.

Das besondere Kennzeichen von Glastonbury ist der 'Tor', ein kegelförmiger Hügel ca. 160 Meter hoch, auf dem der St. Michael Kirchturm steht. Schon der Aussicht wegen lohnt es sich, den Hügel zu besteigen.

In der Nähe von Warminster, im Südosten von Bristol liegt Longleat, das berühmte Heim der Familie Thynne, der Marquis von Bath, denen der Sitz noch heute gehört. Sir John Thynne errichtete den Bau in den 1570er Jahren und seither ist am Aeussern sehr wenig geändert worden. Im Innern herrscht vorallem ein üppiger, italienischer Stil der 1870er Jahre, mit viel feiner Kunstfertigkeit und reich gezierten und farbigen Ausführungen, was einen großartigen Rahmen für die, von der Familie seit 1682 gesammlten fabelhaften Gegenstände, Kunstwerke von höchster Qualität, bildet.

Longleat bietet viele andere Attraktionen, darunter einen Safari-Park mit Löwen.

Corsham, südwestlich von Chippenham, ist eine Stadt reich an verschiedenartigen Gebäuden des 17. und 18. Jahrhunderts, im goldfarbenen Kalkstein gebaut. Ein Besuch lohnt sich.

Corsham Court wurde um 1582 von Thomas Smythe, einem London Zolleinnehmer, gebaut und in 1745 von Paul Methuen übernommen, dessen Nachkommen noch heute dort wohnen. Verschiedene bedeutende Aenderungen haben stattgefunden seit Corsham Court im Besitz der Familie Methuen ist, um passende Räume zur Verfügung zu haben für die hervorragenden, vorallem italienischen und flämischen Gemälde von Malern wie Van Dyck, Rubens, Poussin und Filippo Lippi (Foto Seite 23)

Le point culminant de Glastonbury est le 'Tor' (Massif de roche), une colline conique d'environ 520 pieds de hauteur couronnée par la tour de l'Eglise St. Michael. Il faut absolument y monter si ce n'est que pour admirer la vue.

Près de Warminster, au sud-est de Bristol se trouve Longleat, une magnifique propriété appartenant depuis des siècles à la famille Thynne, Marquis de Bath. La maison fut construite par Sir John Thynne dans les années 1570, et depuis n'a pratiquement pas été modifiée extérieurement. L'intérieur est dans le style opulent italien des années 1870 avec des détails raffinés, élégants et hautement colorés. Cette élégante architecture intérieure procure un magnifique décor pour le prestigieux contenu de la maison, oeuvres d'art de toute sortes et de la plus haute qualité, collectionnées par la famille depuis 1682.

Il y a de nombreuses autres attractions à Longleat y compris le Safari Park et ses lions.

Corsham, au sud-est de Chippenham est une ville riche en monuments variés du XVII et XVIIIème siècle, construits en pierre calcaire locale. Corsham vaut un détour et une visite.

'Corsham Court' (Palais de Corsham) fut construit en 1582 par Thomas Smythe et acquis en 1745 par Paul Methuen dont les descendants en sont encore les propriétaires. La famille Methuen a apporté de nombreuses transformations importantes au palais pour créer des pièces suffisamment grandioses pour recevoir leur impressionnante collection de peintures principalement italiennes et flamandes dont les artistes étaient Van Dyck Rubens, Poussin et Philippo Lippi (Photo de la Galerie des tableaux, page 23).

23

The Abbey and most of the village of Lacock, to the east of Corsham, rightly belong to the National Trust.

The Abbey *(photograph page 24)* is essentially of two periods, its construction as a medieval nunnery and its conversion as a private house in 1540-53. The Abbey was very wealthy and its fifteenth-century cloisters are especially lovely; they surrounded a square court and remain at the centre of the later house. The buildings date mainly from 1232-47 and among their treasures is a huge cauldron cast at Malines in 1500.

The finest feature of later date is the hall which dominates the west front and which was remodelled in 1745-6 by Sanderson Miller for John Ivory Talbot. It is a spectacular room with much early gothic detail, including the plasterwork of the arched ceiling, and houses exaggerated terracotta figures, gesticulating from their niches on the walls, also a set of tables made of yew. The house's most famous nineteenth-century owner was W.H. Fox Talbot, a man of wide-ranging scientific interests, who perfected the calotype photographic process at Lacock in 1840.

Lacock village *(photograph page 24)* is an exceptional and precious survival, full of architectural interest without being overtly pretty. Its days of great prosperity were the fourteenth to sixteenth centuries, but it is only the last 150 years that have left comparatively little mark there.

Castle Combe *(photograph page 25)* is a compact and picturesque village north of Corsham, with a stream flowing through the middle of it. The stone-built houses with their stone-tiled roofs centre upon the medieval Market Cross. Many of them were rebuilt during the tenure as lord of the manor of Sir John Fastolf (the original of Shakespeare's rumbustious Falstaff) in the early fifteenth century, the heyday of the woollen industry; nevertheless, the general appearance of the village is now seventeenth-century.

Das Kloster und der größere Teil des Dorfes Lacock, östlich von Corsham, gehört mit Recht dem 'National Trust'.

Das Kloster (Foto Seite 24) war ursprünglich ein Nonnenkloster, doch wurde es dann von 1540-53 in ein Privathaus umgebaut. Es war ein wohlhabendes Kloster und die Kreuzgänge des 15. Jahrhunderts sind ganz besonders schön. Sie umgaben einen viereckigen Hof und sind im neuen Bau erhalten worden. Die Gebäude datieren besonders von 1232-47 und zu den Schätzen gehört ein mächtiger, in Malines um 1500 gegossener Kessel. Der berühmteste Besitzer dieses Hauses war der im 19. Jahrhundert lebende W.H. Fox Talbot, ein Pionier mit weitgehenden wissenschaftlichen Interessen. Um 1840 vervollkommte er in Lacock die kalotyp-photographische Entwicklung. Lacock (Foto Seite 24) ist ein außerordentliches und wertvolles Dorf der Vergangenheit, voller interessanter Architektur, ohne

eigentlich offenkundig hübsch zu zein.
    Castle Combe (Foto Seite 25) liegt nördlich von Corsham und ist ein festverbundenes, bildschönes Dörfchen, mitten durch welches ein Bach fließt. Die aus Stein gebauten Häuser mit ihren Steinziegeldächern sind um das mittelalterliche Marktplatzkreuz herum zerstreut. Viele davon sind im frühen 15. Jahrhundert während der Besitzzeit des Gutsherrn Sir John Fastolf (Originalfigur für Shakespeares ungestümen Falstaff) neu errichtet worden.

    L'Abbaye et pratiquement tout le village de Lacock à l'est de Corsham, appartiennent au National Trust (Organisme national de conservation).
    L'Abbaye (Photo page 24) date essentiellement de deux périodes. Elle fut édifiée en tant que nonnerie à l'époque médiévale et transformée en maison particulière en 1540-1553. L'Abbaye était très riche et ses péristyles du XVème siècle sont spécialement beaux, ils entourent une cour et sont au centre de la maison actuelle. Les bâtiments datent principalement de 1232-1247 et parmi leurs trésors est un énorme chaudron fondu à Malines en 1500. Monsieur W.H. Fox Talbot physicien réputé fut le propriétaire le plus connu de l'Abbaye, en 1840 il perfectionna à Lacock le procédé photographique sur papier. Le village de Lacock a exceptionnellement bien survécu et est rempli d'intérêts architecturaux sans être trop précieux.
    Castle Combe (Photo page 25) est un village pittoresque au nord de Corsham, traversé par un ruisseau. Les maisons de pierre avec leurs toits en pierre se regroupent autour de la croix médiévale de la Place du Marché. Nombreuses de ces maisons furent reconstruites au début du XVème siècle a l'époque où Sir John Fastolf était chatelain (Fastoft fut le modèle du Falstaff de Shakespeare).

25

Bath is one of the finest eighteenth-century cities in Europe, built around and named after its famed mineral water springs. The restorative and healing powers of drinking and bathing in their waters have attracted men since before the Romans first founded the city as a small spa in the first century A.D. They called it Aquae Sulis, the Waters of Sulis, goddess of the hot springs. After prosperity in the Middle Ages, based on the wool trade, in the eighteenth century the city became fashionable as a spa, frequented by monarchs and high society and graced by the buildings which give the city so much of its present-day appeal.

The Roman Baths are at its centre. The Roman Spa complex is unusually well preserved — the Great Bath *(photograph page 28)* is still lined with the original lead; there are four baths and pools with water of different temperatures and the remains of the hypocaust heating system. The museum houses discoveries made in excavations including a fine and enigmatic gilded bronze head of Minerva. The water should be tasted in the adjacent Pump Room.

The only major reminder of Tudor Bath is the Abbey Church, begun by Bishop Oliver King in 1499. Very prominent on the west front are angels ascending and descending ladders from heaven, representing King's dream, in which a voice prophesied 'let a King restore the church'. He obtained Henry VII's masons Robert and William Vertue to design it, and they promised him vaulting unsurpassed in England or France. The resulting church is expensively conceived and of exceptionally uniform design with fan vaulting throughout, flying buttresses, traceried parapets and a central tower, all built of the finest ashlar.

But Bath is overwhelmingly a Georgian city, effectively built within the century after 1725. This achievement is owed largely to three men. First Beau Nash, the 'King of Bath' who, as

Aerial view of Bath showing Pulteney Bridge, the River Avon & the Abbey

Master of Ceremonies at the baths from 1704, determinedly raised the city's tone and manners, introduced the spirit of elegance, and turned the plain spa (albeit one patronised by Queen Anne) into a society centre. Secondly, Ralph Allen, a local man who had made a fortune from reorganising the nation's postal services, bought the Combe Down quarries in 1727 and made Bath stone famous. But most important of all was John Wood, an architect of vision who settled in Bath in 1727 at the age of twenty-three. He realised the possibility of imposing architectural discipline on whole areas of the city and building so that each house formed part of a grander design. This advance in town planning was unique in Europe, and set a standard which others followed.

Wood built the Circus, in 1754-8, on a virgin site and the earliest circus in England. It is perhaps the most attractive part of Bath with its coupled Doric, Ionic and Corinthian columns applied continuously around the circular shape. Originally it was paved, where now the plane trees grow.

Wood's son John continued to develop Bath from his father's death in 1754 until his own in 1781. He built up a number of streets such as Gay Street, Milsom Street and George Street, linking his father's works one to another, or to the old city. In addition he built Brock Street, which leads without warning into Wood's huge and majestic Royal Crescent, *(photograph page 29)* the first and greatest crescent in England. Built in 1767-75, thirty houses are united by giant Ionic columns in a tremendous arc. No. 1 is open to the public. Wood also built the Assembly Rooms, opened in 1771, the social centre of late eighteenth-century Bath for the well-to-do. Its rooms are superb and the Ball Room and Tea Room rise through two storeys.

Contemporaneously, an equally elegant Banqueting Room was built for the wealthy businessmen of Bath, in the new Guildhall. Its refined plasterwork was designed by Thomas Baldwin in the manner of Robert Adam. Within twenty years

Baldwin also built the Pump Room, a saloon of the greatest elegance, with fine plasterwork and a statue of Beau Nash, and where the mineral waters arrive in a fountain. Adam himself designed Pulteney Bridge to cross the Avon at Bathwick, which Baldwin and others began to develop in 1788. The bridge, conceived in 1770, is named after Sir William Pulteney, and has shops of integral design on both sides of it.

Elsewhere in Bath there are many reminders of the eighteenth century, from the city watchman's stone sentry box in Norfolk Crescent to the natural stone paving and cobbles, the ironwork of balconies and railings, and old lettering and shopfronts. Look out, too, for the tablets to famous former residents such as Gainsborough and Jane Austen.

Bath ist eine der elegantesten 18. Jahrhundert-Städte Europas. Die Stadt erhielt ihren Namen von den berühmten Mineralwasserquellen. Die stärkenden und heilenden Kräfte im Trinken und im Baden dieser Naturquellen zog Menschen nach Bath schon bevor die Römer die Stadt im ersten Jahrhundert n.Chr. gründeten. Mittelpunkt der Stadt sind die Römischen Bäder und der ganze Heilquellenkomplex ist ungewöhnlich gut erhalten (Foto Seite 28) – mit Bädern und Bassins mit Wasser in verschiedenen Temperaturen und Rückständen des unterirdischen Heizung systems. Im Museum kann man Gegenstände sehen, die bei den Ausgrabungen entdeckt worden sind, worunter ein feiner und rätselhafter vergoldeter Bronzekopf der Minerva besonders erwähnenswert ist. Ueber den Bädern liegt Baths gesellschaftlicher Treffpunkt, 'The Pump Room', wo man an einem Brunnen das Mineralwasser versuchen kann. Nebenbei steht die Abtei, das einzige bedeutende Gebäude der Tudor Periode in Bath.

Vorallem ist Bath jedoch eine Stadt des georganischen Zeitalters, die mit Erfolg im Jahrhundert nach 1725 erbaut worden ist. Ihre Bedeutung hat sie vorallem drei Männern zu verdanken. Erstens, 'Beau Nash', dem 'König von Bath', der als Zeremonienmeister in den Bädern nach 1704 mit Entschlossenheit das Niveau und Verhalten der Stadt emporgehoben hat. Er erzeugte Elan und Eleganz und so wurde der einfache Badeort (obwohl von Königin Anne gefördert) zum gesellschaftlichen Mittelpunkt. Dann, Ralph Allen, ein Einheimischer, der durch die Neuorganisation des nationalen Postdienstes sehr wohlhabend geworden war und in 1727 den Steinbruch auf Combe Down kaufte, worauf der Bath-Stein weit und breit bekannt wurde. Am bedeutendsten jedoch war John Wood, ein Architekt mit Einbildungskraft, der sich in 1727 als Dreiundzwanzigjähriger in Bath niederließ. Ihm kam der Gedanke, ganze Gebiete der Stadt architektonisch so zu planen, daß ein jedes Haus Teil eines größeren Entwurfes wurde. In 1754-8 baute er auf unbebautem Land 'The Circus', der erste Bau solcher Art in England. Ursprünglich war der kreisrunde Platz gepflastert, doch heute steht eine Platane in der Mitte.

Nach John Woods Tod wurde seine Arbeit von seinem Sohn John von 1754 weitergeführt bis er im Jahre 1781 starb. Er errichtete Brock Street, die, ohne Warnung, in die von Wood erbaute, gewaltige und majestätische Royal Crescent (Foto Seite 29) führt, die erste und größte halbmondförmige Straße in England. Der Halbkreis besteht aus 30 Häusern, die durch riesige ionische Säulen miteinander verbunden sind. Erbauungszeit war 1767-75. Royal Crescent Nr. 1 steht dem Publikum zur Besichtigung offen.

Die Pulteney Brücke über die Avon bei Bathwick ist von Robert Adam entworfen und von Baldwin und anderen in 1788 ausgebaut worden. Der Bau der Brücke wurde in 1770 erdacht; sie trägt den Name von Sir William Pulteney und hat beiden Seiten entlang Geschäfte. Es gibt vieles was auf das 18. Jahrhundert hinweist in Bath zu sehen. Inschriftstafeln machen den Spaziergänger darauf aufmerksam, daß viele berühmte Leute in dieser Stadt gewohnt haben, wie z.B. Gainsborough und Jane Austen.

Bath est une des plus élégantes cités du XVIIIème siècle en Europe, construite autour et nommée après ses fameuses sources d'eau thermale. Les pouvoirs fortifiants et curratifs de l'**eau** bue ou prise en bain ont attirés les hommes depuis bien avant que les romains ne fondent la ville, au Ier siècle avant Jésus Christ.

Les bains romains sont au centre de la ville. La station thermale datant de l'époque romaine est exceptionnellement bien conservée (Photo page 28) — avec des bains et piscines dont l'eau est à différentes températures et les restes du système de chauffage hypocauste. Le musée contient les découvertes faites lors des fouilles, telle qu'une superbe et énigmatique tête de Minerve en bronze. L'eau doit être goûtée dans la 'Pump Room'. A proximité des bains romains s'élève le seul reste de l'époque tudor à Bath: l'Abbaye.

Bath est essentiellement une cité georgienne construite après 1725. Sa réalisation est largement due à trois hommes. Le premier, 'Beau Nash' surnommé 'Le Roi de Bath' qui en tant que Maitre des Cérémonies aux thermes à partir de 1740 a élevé de façon certaine le ton et les manières de la ville. Il a introduit l'élégance et transformé une station thermale ordinaire (bien que patronnée par la Reine Anne) en centre mondain. Le deuxième était Ralph Allen, un homme local qui avait fait fortune en réorganisant les services postaux de la nation, a acheté les carrières de Combe Down en 1727 et rendit célèbre la pierre de Bath. Mais certainement l'homme le plus important fut John Wood, un architecte qui s'installa à Bath en 1727, à l'age de 23 ans. Il parvint à imposer une discipline architecturale dans des quartiers entiers de la ville et dessina des bâtiments de telle sorte que chaque maison faisait partie d'un ensemble plus important. Woods construit le 'Circus' en 1754-1780, sur un terrain vague, ce fut le premier Circus en Angleterre. A l'origine la partie centrale du Circus où maintenant s'élèvent d'énormes platanes, était pavée.

Le fils de Wood, John continua de développer Bath après la mort de son père en 1754 jusqu'à sa mort en 1781. Il réalisa Brock Street, qui mène à l'énorme et majestueux 'Royal Crescent' (Croissant Royal) (Photo page 29). Le 'Royal Crescent' est le premier et le plus important groupe de maisons en forme de croissant construit en Grande Bretagne. Construit entre 1767 et 1775, trente maisons sont réunies par de géantes colonnes ioniques pour former un arc imposant. La maison qui porte le numéro I est ouverte au public.

Robert Adam a dessiné 'Pulteney Bridge' pour traverser l'Avon à Bathwick. Baldwin a commencé à développer ce pont en 1788. Le pont conçu en 1770 a été nommé après Sir William Pulteney et a des magasins de chaque côté de sa rue. Partout dans Bath on retrouve de nombreux rappels du XVIIème siècle. Ouvrez l'oeil et vous trouverez sur certaines maisons des plaques nommant de célèbres habitants tels que Gainsborough et Jane Austin.

Seven miles north of Bath lies the National Trust property, Dyrham Park, *(photograph page 30)* a handsome stone house set low in a fold of a hill. It was built in two stages, in 1692-1704 by William Blathwayt, who gradually replaced the ancestral home of his wife's family, while continuing its juxtaposition with the medieval church, the two being cleverly linked in one ensemble.

Dyrham is especially interesting for its unity of period; only minor alterations have been made since 1704 and many of William's possessions are retained, giving a very real sense of his taste. His work in the Low Countries as a diplomat and Secretary at War to King William III is reflected in his choice of paintings, many of them contemporary Dutch masterpieces, and his liking for blue and white Delftware, also of Dutch gilt leather hangings. They remain in his splendid rooms, hung with tapestries or lined with panelling of oak, cedar and walnut, or painted in imitation of marble, and in the halls with their cedar and walnut staircases.

The park and gardens were originally laid out by George London but simplified by Humphrey Repton in 1800, when many of the glorious beech, chestnut and Atlantic cedar trees were planted.

At an easy distance north from Dyrham on the A433 is Westonbirt Arboretum, established in the 1860's and containing numerous species of trees and shrubs.

North of Bristol and overlooking the Severn estuary stands Berkeley Castle, *(photograph page 31)* a craggy stone fortress in a wooded and pastoral landscape, where Edward II was imprisoned and murdered and which was stormed by Cromwell's troops. Berkeley Castle was founded by William Fitz Osborn, Earl of Hereford, before 1071, and the mid-twelfth century keep with its Norman doorway is the oldest part remaining.

Berkeley is now essentially a house of 1340-50, built by Thomas Lord Berkeley, heavily castellated and splendidly preserved, with many original features and much beautiful detail, including carved stonework and painted ceilings, and the 'Berkeley arch' with its large cusps. Within, little imagination is required to restore an unusually complete impression of a medieval baron's house, with its great hall and chapel, kitchen and bakehouse, and the private living rooms, many of which still fulfill functions comparable to their original ones. Continuity is supplied by the Berkeley family, who have lived here for eight hundred years, collecting much good furniture and magnificent paintings, tapestries and other heirlooms over the centuries.

A little way up the Severn estuary is Slimbridge, centre of the Wildfowl Trust, and attractively laid out, where a great variety of aquatic and other birds attract enthusiasts from all over England.

11 km nördlich von Bath liegt im Falten eines Hügels Dyrham Park (Foto Seite 30), Besitz des 'National Trusts', ein schönes Haus aus Stein, das von William Blathwayt in 1692-1704 in zwei Zeitabschnitten erbaut worden ist. Dyrham ist besonders wegen seiner Einheitlichkeit im Stil interessant. Seit 1704 sind nur wenig Aenderungen ausgeführt worden und da vieles was William gehörte noch heute vorhanden ist, bekommt man einen wahren Eindruck seines Geschmackes. Der Park und die Gärten wurden von George London entworfen, sind jedoch später um 1800 von Humphrey Repton vereinfacht worden. Er pflanzte herrliche Buchen, Kastanienbäume und atlantische Zedern.

Im Norden von Bristol mit Ueberblick über die Severn Flußmündung liegt das Schloß Berkeley (Foto Seite 31), eine felsige Steinfestung in waldiger und ländlicher Umgebung. Hier wurde Eduard II ins Gefängnis geworfen und ermordet; auch ist die Festung von Cromwells Truppen bestürmt worden. Berkeley ist jetzt vorallem ein Haus aus den Jahren 1340-50, von Thomas Lord Berkeley erbaut. Innerhalb des Schlosses kann man ohne Schwierigkeiten einen ungewöhnlich vollständigen Einblick in ein mittelalterliches Baronenhaus bekommen mit der großen Halle and Kapelle, Küche und Bäckerei, den privaten Wohnzimmern, wovon einige noch heute zu Zwecken dienen, die mit den ursprünglichen vergleichbar sind.

A sept milles au nord de Bath se trouve Dyrham Park, une propriété appartenant au National Trust. C'est une majestueuse maison en pierre de Bath nichée dans un creux de la colline. Elle fut construite en deux étapes, de 1692 a 1704 par William Blathwayt. Dyrham est spécialement intéressante à cause de son unité dans sa construction. Trés peu de transformations ont été apportées à la maison depuis 1704, à l'intérieur on trouve de nombreuses possessions de William Blathwayt donnant un aperçu de son goût véritable. Le park et les jardins furent à l'origine dessinés par George London mais simplifiés par Humphrey Repton en 1800, lorsque de magnifiques hêtres, des marronniers et des cèdres de l'atlantique furent plantés.

Au nord de Bristol et dominant l'estuaire de la Severn s'élève 'Berkeley Castle' (Château de Berkeley) (Photo page 31) une forteresse escarpée dans un paysage boisé et de pâturages où fut emprisonné et assassiné Edouard II. Ce château fut également pris d'assaut par les troupes de Cromwell. Berkeley construit par Thomas Lord Berkeley en 1340-1350 est maintenant principalement une maison. A l'intérieur il faut peu d'imagination pour restaurer l'impression complète d'une maison d'un baron médieval, avec sa grande salle et sa chapelle, sa cuisine, son four à pain et les salons privés qui à l'heure actuelle son encore utilisés pour des receptions.

31

In & Around BRISTOL

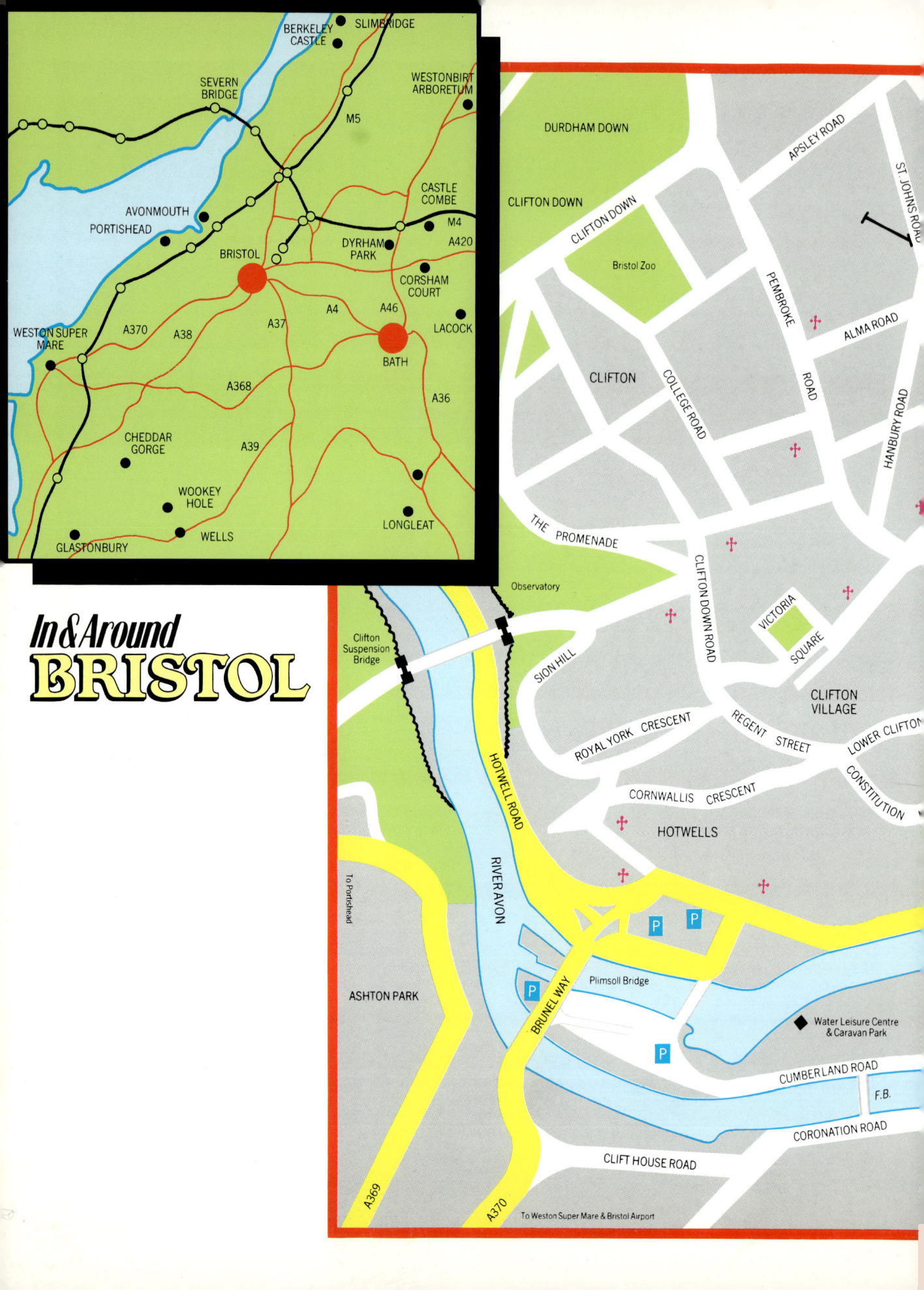